simply romantic®

tips to

ROMANCE

your husband

Foreword by Barbara Rainey

FamilyLife Publishing®
Little Rock, Arkansas

Tips to Romance Your Husband
FamilyLife Publishing®
5800 Ranch Drive
Little Rock, Arkansas 72223
1-800-FL-TODAY • FamilyLife.com
FLTI, d/b/a FamilyLife®, is a ministry of Campus Crusade for Christ International®

© 2005, 2014 FamilyLife

ISBN: 978-1-60200-709-3

Printed in the United States of America

Second Edition

20 19 18 17 16   1 2 3 4 5

CONTENTS

FOREWORD

Dry-erase markers, coupons, puzzle pieces, and chocolates . . . this little book is packed with innovative ideas to help you communicate love to your sweetheart.

Creatively expressing love involves forethought and planning. Let's face it, most of us could use some inspiration to spark romance—Simply Romantic® *Tips to Romance Your Husband* is packed with ideas that will help you demonstrate love to your husband.

Sometimes even the smallest gesture can say, "I love you." Take the time to show him that you notice him and know what he likes. Your beloved will be encouraged . . . your friendship will be strengthened . . . and romance will blossom.

Barbara Rainey

Barbara Rainey
Cofounder of FamilyLife®
Mother of six and grandmother of numerous grandchildren

ROMANTIC MESSAGES

Write him a check for one hundred kisses.
Be available to cash the check for him when
and where he pleases.

2

Buy your guy a leather-bound journal and write inspirational and romantic quotes, thoughts, and love notes for him. As you journey through life together, continue adding new thoughts that affirm your love and respect for him.

Create a special—and unusual—place in the
house to make love. Leave little Post-it notes
throughout the house leading your husband to
your special love nest.

Before your next day at the beach,
prepare a special message in a bottle for your
loved one. Hide it in a place where the two of
you will come across it as you lead
him on a walk.

Write a message to your husband on card stock, and cut it into five puzzle pieces. For four continuous days, mail him one of the pieces. On the fifth day reveal when and where he should meet you to get the final piece of the puzzle.

Leave a note in his car that says, "I can't wait to see you tonight" ... or maybe ... "I can't wait for you to see me tonight!" Then wear something to bed that catches his eye.

Send a sexy e-mail or text message
to your man.

8

When your husband goes out of town,
give him a sealed note for each day he will be
gone. Build anticipation in each note
for his return home.

The next time you're out to dinner, casually take out a pen and write a note to him on a paper napkin—letting him know what he can look forward to at home. Fold it and slide it across the table.

Compliment your husband in front of others—especially your kids. You may be the only one in his life who's doing it!

11

Using dry-erase markers, leave a note
to your sweetie on the bathroom mirror.

12

On a small piece of paper,
write a short note of encouragement
and slip it into his pants pocket.
He'll find it later when he's fishing
for change.

13

Send a bouquet of candies or cookies
to his workplace with a sweet note.

Compose a love poem for your love.
Find a special time and place to read it to
him. Consider framing it and hanging
it in your bedroom.

ROMANTIC TOUCH

15

Does he play on an intramural team
or in an adult league? At his next game, or
just the next time he goes to the
driving range or the bowling alley,
go along and cheer him on.

16

Treat your hardworking honey to a back rub.

Dust off that old game of Twister and have some fun! With each round, the loser must remove a piece of clothing. He'll be sure to see that you lose.

18

Join him the next time he's taking a
shower. Too shy? Then greet your guy with
a warm towel as he's stepping out of the
shower and help him dry off.

19

As he heads out for work, give him a
passionate kiss. If he wants to know what it
was for—tell him it's the appetizer
for tonight's menu.

20

Go for a walk after dinner holding hands.

Spend time kissing him—*really* kissing him.

Play footsie with him the next time
you are having dinner with your in-laws.

23

When the house is quiet—light some
candles—play some soft music—and
dance cheek to cheek. Make it a
dance he will never forget!

24

The next time your husband is at the kitchen sink, walk up behind him and give him a really big hug.

Pamper your husband with a relaxing foot massage. All you need is a warm basin of water, some soap, a towel, and some lotion.

26

On a chilly night, cuddle under
a blanket with your husband and
watch a movie. Surprise him with a
little kiss on the lips or nip
on the neck.

27

Get up a few minutes earlier than usual, brush
your teeth, then get back in bed and wake
him up with a kiss.

Play the "Touching Game."
Make 10 cards describing
"Ways to Touch"—and 10 cards with
"Places to Touch" (one idea per card).
Without looking, pull one card from
each pile and then take action.

ROMANTIC GIFTS

29

Save your spare change in a large, clear jar.
Let him know you are saving up to buy
him something special.

30

Make him a book of coupons that are good for things he likes: his favorite dessert, a special meal, and you.

Bring him a surprise from the grocery
store—a magazine, a candy bar, or
anything else—that will let him know
you were thinking about him.

Buy him that CD, DVD, book,
or video game that he's had his eye on.

33

Keep a running list of his favorite things,
clothes sizes, and gift ideas. (See the appendix
for special charts.)

34

Go with him to his favorite store—
and let him treat himself to something he'd like.

Secretly buy him tickets to a special event.
Plan a lunch/dinner date on the day of the
event. After dessert, give him the tickets.

Purchase a piece of clothing for yourself
that you know he will especially like. Pick a
special time and place to wear it!

37

If your husband is a collector of coins,
baseball cards, etc., buy him something that
adds to his collection.

Have a professional photographer take a picture
of you. Frame your favorite pose and
give it to your husband.

Refrain from saying, "I told you so."
That might be the best gift of all.

Find a used bookstore or check online
for a collectible copy of his favorite book.

41

Handwrite his favorite Bible verse on parchment. After laminating it, surprise him by tucking it into his Bible.

42

For a significant anniversary—buy him
a gold watch. Engrave it with a romantic
phrase like "I'll always have time for you."

ROMANTIC MOMENTS

43

Arrange for you and your spouse to take a
day off—and then do something
you enjoy together.

Schedules can often get out of control. Be sure to schedule time just for yourself, so you will have some energy left for him.

45

Serve him his favorite dessert and gourmet
coffee—by candlelight.

Take the afternoon off and catch a matinee.
Sit in the back row!

Play a board game you both enjoy.

Sit down with your husband and listen
to him. Ask him how you can help
fulfill the dreams he has for his life.

49

Reminisce about your favorite dating
memories. Plan together to
reproduce his favorite one.

50

Pick up the book *Rekindling the Romance* (ShopFamilyLife.com) and tell him you'd like to read it together.

Go to a local park.
Spend some time reconnecting as a couple.
Pack snacks and stay awhile.

Have your guy write down on
slips of paper his five favorite things to do.
Fold them and place them in a bowl. Let
him draw one out and read it—then make
plans to do it together.

53

Circle and star a location on a map,
then tape the map to the fridge. When he
asks, just smile and wink—but don't tell.
On the appointed day, drive him to the
location and either have a picnic
or just make out.

54

Play a spicy rendition of the old classic childhood game of "Mother, May I?" Change the name to "Darling, May I?" and have lots of grown up fun.

Blindfold your husband and kidnap him.
Take him to a hotel room where you have
prepared a romantic tryst.

56

Take a class together. Find a topic, hobby, or sport you both want to learn more about—and sign up!

Spend time together in the kitchen making
his favorite dinner, cookies, or dessert.

Prepare a special snack at bedtime
and serve it to him in bed. Chocolate
covered anything is sure to please!

ROMANTIC MOVES

59

Wash and vacuum his car.
For the final touch—top off his gas tank, too.

60

Tell your husband you'd like to start exercising together so that you'll both be around to enjoy each other longer.

Pick up his favorite dish from his
favorite restaurant and serve it to him on
your best china.

62

Host a party for him and his friends
to watch their favorite sporting event on TV.

63

Give him a break from his weekend
chores by either mowing the lawn or
arranging for it to be done.

64

Drop by your husband's
workplace unexpectedly and whisk him
away for lunch.

65

Initiate something special in the bedroom.

66

You are never too old to flirt.
Flirt with the man you married.

67

Surprise your husband with a special "spa treatment" after he's had a long, hard day at work. Draw him a bath and create a soothing environment—scented candles, bubbles, music, refreshing beverage, etc.

Think of a couple of things that your honey does for you and the family (he is a good provider, he can fix things, etc.) and let him know how much you appreciate him.

69

On Friday night—tell him he gets to
sleep late the next morning. Serve
him breakfast in bed.

Offer to shave him. (If you think
there is any chance you might
accidentally cut him, then
offer to wash his hair.)

71

Plan a weekend away for the two of you.
Cater to his desires and his needs.

72

The next time he's watching a game on
television, ask him if he has any plans
for halftime. If not, tell him you've
made plans for him to score.

Prepare for special events:
Maintain current e-mail addresses and cell
phone numbers of your husband's friends. You
may want to throw him a surprise birthday
party or plan a celebration when
he accomplishes something significant.

74

Hire a handy man to fix things around the house. Use the time you saved your hubby to do something fun together.

ROMANTIC ADVICE

75

If your lives are crazy busy,
schedule some special time for romance
on your calendars. Use little red heart
stickers to mark the days.

76

Men are stimulated by sight—
take a personal interest in your appearance.

Let the last words he hears
each night be, "I love you."

Admit when you're wrong and be willing to say,
"I'm sorry, will you forgive me?"

79

Consider attending a Weekend to Remember® marriage getaway. Visit FamilyLife.com/Weekend.

Remember:
"The older the violin, the sweeter the music."
(author unknown)

Choose a poem, scripture passage,
or lyrics from a favorite song to read to
your husband at bedtime.

82

Instead of feeling frustrated when he forgets to put the toilet seat down, thank him when he remembers.

83

On occasion, wear his favorite perfume—
even if it is not *your* favorite.

Be a student of your spouse. Know his
likes and dislikes, his strengths and
weaknesses, and his fears.

Keep your bedroom well stocked
with candles, romantic cards, massage oil,
bubble bath, chocolate, etc.

Men view romance differently from women.
Ask your husband to describe what's romantic
to him. Don't be surprised when his ideas
sound very different from yours.

87

Pray for your husband every day.

ROMANTIC HOLIDAYS & SPECIAL DAYS

88

On New Year's Day, whisper in his ear that you are
determined to find some new places to kiss him.
When you're alone with him, start to make
good on your promise.

Tell your husband that you will be treating him to an off-season baseball game for Valentine's Day. Then, in your bedroom or some other private location, lead him through first base, second base, third base, and then bring him in for a home run.

90

Sleep in, have breakfast in bed, and watch the Groundhog Day prediction together. If the groundhog sees his shadow, unveil your six-week plan for staying warm.

91

Fill several Easter eggs with notes telling
your husband why you love him. Nestle the
eggs in a decorated basket.

92

The next time you and your spouse
attend a wedding, tell him, "If I had it to do
all over, I'd marry you again." Enjoy a second
honeymoon after the reception.

Have fun foolin' around on April Fool's Day.
Share an umbrella, roll up your jeans, and splash in
the puddles *sans galoshes*.

94

Father's Day is a great day to celebrate with
your husband. Rent a convertible for the day
and drive around with the top down.

95

The 19th of October is Sweetest Day.
Ask his mother or sibling to list his favorite
candies from childhood. Purchase these
nostalgic goodies as a special
gift for your sweetie.

On Thanksgiving Day, give him a
handwritten letter with the reasons you are
thankful that he is yours for life.

97

Make a point of jotting down a few traits
or actions everyday that make you respect
and desire your husband. On your next
date night, present him with the list or
read it aloud to him.

Spice up the "Twelve Days of Christmas." Each day from December 25 through January 5 create small, personal gifts (notes, snacks, yourself!) for him only. January 6 buy a King's Cake, or make your own, to close out the Christmas season.

Celebrate his birthday at the office
with cake and ice cream for everyone.

100

Plan a romantic birthday surprise.
Book the honeymoon suite at your favorite hotel,
and buy him a special gift—
something that will spice up the evening.

101

Make your own holiday! Take this
opportunity to create a holiday that is special
and unique to the two of you.

APPENDIX

Sizes for Him:

Jeans: _____

Slacks: _____

Shirt: _____

Shoes: _____

Ring: _____

Other: _____

_____

GIFT LIST